THOUGHTS ON CRASHING

Thoughts on Crashing

Bob Garot

Copyright © 2014 Bob Garot
All rights reserved.

First published: August 2014

Designed by Valentina Pagliai

Published by Hudson Writers
North Plainfield, NJ 07060
United States of America

ISBN: 1941997007
ISBN-13: 978-1-941997-00-0

To Vale

CONTENTS

Thoughts on Crashing

Thoughts on Crashing	3
The Dead Gymnast	5
I Marvel	7
Chests Ache Tonight	9
The View from NPI	11
For Steve Sax	13
A Need, a Loneliness, a Desire	15
At the Pass	17
Yours is the World	19
On a Bus in LA	21

On the Slightest Breeze	23
Alone in an Empty Dorm Lounge	25
Wandering	27
Somewhere	29
Thoughts Lost on Awakening	31
Placing the Glass to Her Lips	33

Festering Memories

Festering Memories	37
So What is That?	39
Time Is	41
Juggernaut Coffee	43
Pappy's Lies	45
We Need a Day of the Dead	47
To the Sky, the Void Seems to be Sleeping	49
Over the Bay Bridge	51

The Ocean Churns Its Products	53
I Dreamed	55
Who Assists the Abuser?	57
Saturday Poured Like a Slow Tonic	59
A Friend Dies on His Bed	61
Love Skips Out	63
A Gentle Swagger	65
A Ghost in My House	67
The Loss of My Sister	69
The Amish in Me	71
I Am a—	73
Is Not on the Agenda	75
In This House There is a Room	77
The Knot	79
What Was That	81
Hallmark Cards for the Disenchanted	83
The Bass Resonates	85
What is Our Model for How the	87

World Should Be?

The Intuit*	89
A Dialogue Between the Holy Spirit (HS) and God (G)	91
PCH	93
Just One Jump!	95
The Runaway Bestseller	97
Rain on Friday	99
Where I Find Passion	101
Harvey Molotch Said	103
About the Author	105
Index	107

THOUGHTS ON CRASHING

Thoughts on crashing

On I-5 past midnight
a desert of blackness
subsumes my car and
clouds the eyes.

Dashed lines guide momentum,
disturbing boundlessness with yellow perforations.

Night folds onto itself,
an origami of the mind.

THE DEAD GYMNAST

Her body lay on the cold steel table
    like a broken bird.

I want to run my fingers over her
    in homage to this divinity.

Even in death, there must be so much
    this body can do—a lightness, a
    stretch—so much to wonder at
    without committing the sacrilege
    of opening the skin.

But this is my job, and so I
    pick up my scalpel
    and cut.

I marvel

at the endless efforts

to conjure an aftermath

to the sweet oblivion

and utter finitude

of death.

Chests ache tonight
in this longing city of elegiac desire.
Tragedies turned bittersweet.

Restlessly moving the days' barcodes over
the optical scanner's eye.
How does your local cashier keep from weeping?

Shadows of flickering candles dance
through windows onto pavement.
Obscured now by passing headlights.

THE VIEW FROM NPI*

Death hounds
Our local arcade
Down the street,
Where a fat guy sits reading comics
In a glass cage,
Divvying quarters.

Laugh tracks and
Things explode
On TV tonight.

Students
Roam by outside screaming obscenities,
Puking.

And inside,
We draw pictures
And smile.

* UCLA Neuropsychiatric Institute.

FOR STEVE SAX
*Useless regrets pour like sunshine
on this lost day.*

Stultified with reflexion
Self-immolating
Words despaired on uttering
A throw to first in the stands
And the fans grab their throats,
Tongues out and eyes bulging in glee.

O how to fix it?
Such a simple thing, this 10-yard
Toss of a little hard ball.
Every expert comes to help
But with more talk is more
Reflexion is more pain.
The ball flies into the dugout.

You throw your glove down.
"This is not me!" is implied.
Yet while we mock you, Steve,
Know we love you. Your failure
Is the beginning of
Philosophy,
Art,
And poetry.

A need, a loneliness, a desire.
A noticing, a chemistry, a talk.
A date.

A watchfulness, an anxiety, a self-loathing.
A divorce, a bankruptcy, a grief.

Another disappointment. Fat heartache.

A need, (repeat)

At the pass
The man asked
What was my mistake?
Is there another path
I ought to take?

Facing the ennui
Of goals fulfilled
She leapt precariously
Into another
Awkward beginning.

Yours is the world
  And all that's in it.

So hard to end,
  once you begin it.

Be there and see there
  the lies left to learn.

In the old story
  of loves' labor's burn.

On a bus in LA

bodies jostle

in awkward hallow space

fixed

in glimmering pools

of tears.

On the slightest breeze
A rattling of leaves
Whispers sadness
To passersby
In suit and tie.

We were only fifteen…

I knew the money was gone when…

If I could just afford a drink…

Full of such stories,
The city ignores them.

Ask the leaves.

Alone in an empty dorm lounge in Canada, stretched on a couch as the sky darkens. I read *Harper's* and eat a dinner of oatmeal cookies and mango fruit juice left behind by those who left when the convention finished.

If I fell in here while standing on the dresser to turn the knob for the blinds that lack their wand, how long before someone would find me?
If I somehow end up in a ditch off the road, would I still make it home?
How do I manage, during a ninety-minute presentation, not to get up and sing?

Wandering
Souls recognized
Words comingling
On a warm couch
  with coffee.

How?
Yet somehow
Why not?
Aloneness isn't onlyness
Isn't holiness isn't wholeness.

Past lapses.
Only now.
Only here.
Only us.

Somewhere

Beneath the issues
Outside of schedules
As an undercurrent of relationships

Is a sympathy

At the core of anger
Belying dismissiveness
Always seeking warmth.

Thoughts lost on awakening
Big shadows from my moving pen
I dream in sensible confusions,
Tasty and colorful

On a cliff over the ocean
I am anxious,
Not knowing what the present means,
    Or why it concerns us.

Placing the glass to her lips
She pours the crystalline fluid into herself
To splash over the need in her chest,
The rocking, aching sympathy.

Soft and worried like a child,
Moving, struggling through adulthood,
Settling down, becoming weak, dying.

She places the drink back on the table,
Glad for the glistening

Notes of birds, the still morning air,
Another day to imagine into life.

FESTERING MEMORIES

Festering memories
Bad habits disguised
Old angers and lusts
Stolen kisses and accidents
Earnest betrayals.

No lies hide us from reckonings.
Like Rome, we build ourselves
From past refuse and glory
Constantly simmering, churning
Illogically compelling.

What do we do with so many layers
So many days
Enslaving and releasing.

So what is that?
A lost cigarette
A trumpet with sticky valves
Dirty socks in the corner
A cold wind off the balcony
A half-lit room
A forced smile (of over-acquaintance)
Twelve hours of labor
A stiff neck
A listless Sunday
Mail returned
Indentations on furniture
Distant laughter
Irremovable stains
Out of gas
Heat
loosening
      easing
           to melt.

Time is:

<u>Watching</u>
           <u>A</u>
                    <u>New</u>
                              <u>Moment</u>

Happening
      Cautiously lowered body
            Jazz
                        Here.

Before me
      Learns relaxing languidly
            Shocked Reality
                        Was just

Is made was
      In hot, angry
            Forgot boredom
                        When I said,

      Spa bubbles,
                        "Now."

Juggernaut coffee
Compels me, nervously,
Nauseously intense,
Speaking loudly, fidgeting,
My breath like dead rats,
I become analytical, judgmental—
More like you.

PAPPY'S LIES

We're watching a *Bonanza* episode where a little kid thinks an old bandit is God. "That kid'll be pretty confused," I say. "Aren't we all," says Pappy, well into his eighties.

Then we watched *The Big Valley*. A man said to another that he didn't want to be forgiven, just excused. "Can't do neither," Pappy said. "Once a word is said, it's always out there. People might say they forgive you, but they'll remember it in the back of their heads." He tapped at his bald, pink scalp. "An' it'll come back some day. You can't take nothing back."

Mammie lies in the farthest corner of the house from Pappy's TV, and reads her mystery novels and naps to get off her legs, burdened with poor circulation. She doesn't cook or clean for him anymore, and they don't share the bed where they conceived.

Later I dreamed of going with Pappy, on a train and by foot, to a Jane Fonda resort consisting of three or four gift shops. As we walked he offered me pure water and a sweet cob of corn.

We need a day of the dead
A laughing jackal
Floor 13 in hotels
Rooms without nightlights
Deaths without funerals
Ugly celebrities
Classes for children on hatred and discord
To grow up
To wake up to pain, death, suffering
In our own eyes
Not lies
Not smiles
Not friendly parasites.

To the sky, the void seems to be sleeping.
To the earth, the sky seems to be sleeping.
To the plants, the earth seems to be sleeping.
To the animals, the plants seem to be sleeping.
To humans, the animals seem to be sleeping.
To philosophers, humans seem to be sleeping.
To the void, philosophers seem to be sleeping.

Over the Bay Bridge
Smoking Buddha Cloves
"Roll your window down,
Those make me sick!" she says.
They do me too, and I enjoy
The cold blast on my face
As I force the Buddy Guy tape into the machine and he
Tells me, "Since my woman left me,
Ain't had nothin' but the blues."
"Oh, sing it Buddy," I say.
"Are you sure we're going the
Right way?" she turns it down.
I turn it up, watching enlarging Coke signs
And Reno signs of the San Francisco
Skyline in the holidays, fancying myself
Feelin' Groovy.

She's putting on make-up now,
And says, "It's two and Bob's nearly out
Of bed." I think to ask her how
We discussed each others' traits
Last night Virginia Wolfe style on that bridge,
But we don't need that stress this
Morning. It was something about
Her inflexibility, my murkiness,
Our power struggle. She setting
Agendas, angry when I lead, & I'm sure
She feels the same about me. With
Intense contact, others—anybody—gets
Despicable. When does one get time off
    from a marriage?

The ocean churns its products
    and remorse.
A backdrop for lovers and loners,
playing an endless hymn,
thumping primal rhythms,
flowing like sand
sensitive to the moon's
meek tuggings.
Bearing our filth,
spoiling our surfers,
washing over cinematic kisses
and fateful invasions.
A relentless reminder.

I dreamed I was in a large Chinese amphitheater where rows of cushy seats stood within a few inches of water, which vibrated as music played. It was so soothing I nearly fell asleep—what would have happened if I had?

Who assists the abuser?
Who aids the victimizer?
Who helps the scandalizer?
Who are the innocent accomplices to evil?
Who comforts those pitiful forces
  that cannot cure themselves?

Where are the medals for
  accessories to loneliness?
  accessories to willfulness?
Used life turning raw.

Saturday poured like a slow tonic
   on the week's pain
As I enshrouded myself in thick
   blankets for multiple naps
Caught myself smiling in salsa class
Bundled the newspapers
Washed my clothes.
Tears came at times
For manifold unknown reasons
Which I didn't ponder too long
I lit a candle,
Read the news.

And there are nights
When I remember
   the feeling of this life
The secret spirituality under
   a full moon
The manic excitement of creating,
   refining and enlarging a story
The quiet glee in relishing a
   pretty song or poem
And the desire to create
   new sweet worlds.

A friend dies on his bed with a
   needle in his arm.
A lover tells me, "You're going to
   jail," and picks up the phone to
   call.
My wife sits on the floor crying as I
   pack boxes.

How dreamlike this life is.
Hazy recollections of mornings and meals and work:
   trinkets, mementos, the writing and photos gently
   fading until we see only emptiness, the rest random
      motions,
   grappling in the twilight for food, sex, goods.

Love skips out
Like an awkward relative
   to smoke filterless cigarettes
   on the back porch
Like an impetuous boy
   stealing candy from a liquor store
Like an aging actress
   turned down after another audition.

I drive away in my car
With the radio off
A woman being towed passes
   in the other lane
Then another, with a face
      fraught with despair.

A gentle swagger
Knowingly
A smirk
Not suffering fools
Takes no umbrage

And he is wounded,
Shot down
Sisyphus smiles
Icarus laughs
Silly fatal independence,
Head in palms,
Finds consolation in
That Continuing
        Obscure
    Violent
            Torn
        Heartbreaking
                Vision.

A ghost in my house.
Paper from past lives
Piles like Fall leaves,
Browning with age,
Gently giving their nutrients
   back to the carpet.

The loss of my sister
Is a loss of the ability
To talk about those memories
Only we had together

What becomes of the unshared
    past?

THE AMISH IN ME

Life should come with a label:
Best used when simple.
After hours of good work,
There is good food,
   good talk
   good sex
No entertainment or games,
No friends' excited calls,
No feeling of being in the center
Or, God forbid, on top of things.

So I can sleep satisfied,
With a kind heart
   and a sense of mystery.

I am a—
You are my—
Symphony Rider

Riding on
The ways of
Love's crashing sounds

In deserts
In mountains
I am beside her

She moves me
Into realms
Sacred, profound

In the vast and thoughtful gaze of your eyes
I see the recklessness in the ways that I abide
And the will to have a different way of being free
Is a side of satisfaction that I couldn't see.

You have come, incited to my forest door
I will show you paths and trees, but there is ever more
And if you truly love the ways that I abide
What becomes of all the places where we used to hide?

Is not on the agenda,
Is not an action item
Is not on near inside nor
   outside "the box"
Is not on one's lips like a song
Nor on one's mind like a box score
And is washed off one's body like
   the day's dust.

In this house there is a room
    where all the keys are laid
To change the walls and move
    the doors and maybe
        wake the maid.

For this room I've searched
        and searched
    but I have yet to find
Whether it sits behind my desk
    or a recess of my mind.

Once I find it, you will see
    all this house could ever be.
But for now the walls and doors
        are such
And waiting for that magic
        clutch of keys.

THE KNOT

They brought in a psychic who, strangely enough, looked at the knot in the cord used to pull the sash up at the bedroom window.
"Here it is," she said.
"What?"
"The metaphor, the symbol. It's all around us, but especially apparent here."
"What?"
"The knot. It keeps the sash from hanging fully, and lets the sun in. Even when you don't want it."
"So?"
"You know what I'm talking about. It's all around you. You've created a world of knots."
"Really?"
"The knot surely formed over many months. God knows how it came to bind itself. It has a partner working against its better interests. That other is itself. It's always this. Nothing else knows how to bind so well."

What was that
   idea I had once?
That brilliant one,
That would save so many
And I'd never have to work again.

Was it a design
Or a song
Or a manifesto?

I remember now—
The next day it was banal
Millions of others thought so too
Before and after, through and through
and I couldn't be a martyr for my cause.

HALLMARK CARDS FOR THE
~ DISENCHANTED ~

Congratulations on finding out
that the only person
who can tolerate you
(Inside:) Is a person you find intolerable.

Congratulations on your new job!
(Inside:) Enjoy the rest of your life
as an indentured servant.

Congratulations Graduate!
(Inside:) The fun part's over.

Congratulations on your wedding!
(Inside:) And the legal obligation
to never desire another human being
ever again.

Congratulations on your new baby!
(Inside:) Now you'll know first-hand
the joy of six or more filthy diapers a day.

So sorry for the death of your _____.
But on the bright side,
you don't have to deal with
their shit anymore.

The bass resonates
Its richness into music.
I prefer it played slow
      with a perfect rhythm
      filling every beat in time
      until the cup of love overflows
      with its warmth, and even
      then it continues, its voluminous
      waves surging into your
      cavernous depths, its excesses
      the gift of your patient love.

It rises and falls, catching you, turning
      and twisting like a semi out of
      control. Yet it stays on the road,
      driving forward and bringing all
      the other sounds and jolts which
      awaken and surprise. It veers,
      it swerves, bolts forward and turns
      again, through the heights of a phrase
      to the depths of a passage,
      resounding.

What is our model for how the world should be?
Can we achieve it in an SUV?
Will we find it more easily by bombing Iraq
Or by saturating the inner-city with crack?

Garbage piles up in the streets.
Campagne glasses go "clink" in the suites.
The World Bank will not forgive their debt.
So more immigrants arrive on our doorsteps yet.

And now we wonder, where has winter gone?
All that consumption gone terribly wrong.
Pacific islands disappear, you say, "shit happens."
What will you say when it's downtown Manhattan?

THE INTUIT*

The Intuit* is a device which objectively measures the degree of negative energy in a relationship. Everyone online with The Intuit* has all their vital signs monitored to take that problematic subjectivity out of the subjective. The Intuit* will read the Intuit* levels of any other Intuit* unit within prespecified coordinates, say 5 feet. The self reading will then be matched with the "other" reading to determine the degree of positive or negative energy. With the readout in hand, corrective steps can be taken, which are delineated in a handbook. To help you have that ideal relationship.

This data is collected and stored permanently in FBI vaults, to provide an index of the times. One year is compared to the next, and trends are spotted, worried over and cultivated. Some begin to use The Intuit* to strategically elicit negative readings from the other, or bring down states.

Your TV will automatically adjust to your Intuit* level, as a mood modulator. Those who are depressed will watch "the healing channel," featuring noted shrinks, aerobics, and feel good movies like *It's a Wonderful Life*. More people have killed themselves watching it than any other station.

A DIALOGUE BETWEEN THE HOLY SPIRIT (HS) AND GOD (G)

HS: Are you sure about this "hell" business? Maybe we should rethink that.
G: On what grounds?
HS: Are you sure people should be blamed for their sins? There's cultural variation, genetic defects, chemical imbalances, peer group influences, good days/bad days, bad training, lack of opportunities, etc. Should we impose eternal torment nonetheless?
G: Sure.
HS: OK then!

PCH

curves relentlessly
in 2nd gear swoops
by drooping Redwoods
in the face of angry RVs
as the ocean looms
just over the knoll,
past burdens.

JUST ONE JUMP!

Before you go, daddy,
My daughter told me this morning
As I was trying to pull myself away.

She stood at the edge of the mat,
And off she flew
Like the faery of her dreams
Who leads wolves to do good things in all the world,
Seeing how far she might push my pride and
annoyance
My hurried joy.

THE RUNAWAY BESTSELLER

"Guess it couldn't handle the pressure,"
My sister told me with a laugh,
As we sat watching TV together one afternoon,
With nothing better to do
Than draw mustaches on the faces in the TV Guide,
And be together.

Rain on Friday
Bought a coffeemaker
Saturday I went to see Spence.
Walked to Washington Square Park and
Listened to the bongos.
The park was like a radio
Each corner staked out:
Sitars at one point
Trumpets at another
Rappers at another.
Talked about the economy, the
Men's group, relationships.
We'd both read the same
Article in the New Yorker on
Bill Clinton.
& we walked
Through Little Italy
& Chinatown
Past a million people
And a thousand shops
Full of color.

And in the morning I got up
And walked down to Socrates
Park to find they were celebrating
Their 20th anniversary.
And next door at another park
Were the Indians

With samosas, rice
And beautiful music.
I bought some ripe plums and
Ate them
At the riverbank
Looking over the whole City
Not so intimidating
Just waiting
For us.

Where I find passion
I leave pieces of my life,
Burdened in the darkened woods.

Harvey Molotch said his hairdresser told him,
"How can you have a disappointment
If you don't have an appointment?"

ABOUT THE AUTHOR

Bob Garot grew up on the fringe of the Mojave Desert and now spends his free time jogging in the Tuscan countryside. *Thoughts on Crashing* (1993-1997) were written as he experienced a career change, a divorce, a bankruptcy, both parents having cancer, his sister dying, his best friend dying, his grandmother dying, and his dog dying. In the second section, *Festering Memories* are excerpts from his personal diary between 1987 and 2012.

INDEX

Poems in Alphabetic Order

A Dialogue Between the Holy Spirit (HS) and God (G)	91
A Friend Dies on His Bed	61
A Gentle Swagger	65
A Ghost in My House	67
Alone in an Empty Dorm Lounge	25
A Need, a Loneliness, a Desire	15
At the Pass	17
Chests Ache Tonight	9
Festering Memories	37
For Steve Sax	13
Hallmark Cards for the Disenchanted	83
Harvey Molotch Said	103
I Am a—	73
I Dreamed	55
I Marvel	7
In This House There is a Room	77

Is Not on the Agenda	75
Juggernaut Coffee	43
Just One Jump!	95
Love Skips Out	63
On a Bus in LA	21
On the Slightest Breeze	23
Over the Bay Bridge	51
Pappy's Lies	45
PCH	93
Placing the Glass to Her Lips	33
Rain on Friday	99
Saturday Poured Like a Slow Tonic	59
Somewhere	29
So What is That?	39
The Amish in Me	71
The Bass Resonates	85
The Dead Gymnast	5
The Intuit*	89
The Loss of My Sister	69

The Ocean Churns Its Products	53
The Runaway Bestseller	97
The View from NPI	11
The Knot	79
Thoughts Lost on Awakening	31
Thoughts on Crashing	3
Time Is	41
To the Sky, the Void Seems to be Sleeping	49
Wandering	27
We Need a Day of the Dead	47
What is Our Model for How the World Should Be?	87
Who Assists the Abuser?	57
What Was That	81
Where I Find Passion	101
Yours is the World	19

Notes

Notes

Notes

ps

Notes

Notes

www.ingramcontent.com/pod-product-compliance
Lightning Source LLC
Chambersburg PA
CBHW061329040426
42444CB00011B/2840